David A. Ryan

GWYNN'S ISLAND

VIRGINIA

A History and Pictorial Essay

Written and Illustrated by
David D. Ryan

Resting, Gwynn's Island

For Emily

And the people of Gwynn's Island

Acknowledgements

I have sought through this book to bring to the readers some of the history and charm of Gwynn's Island. Through walks on the beaches with my daughters, Jenny and Emily, and talks with islanders, I have learned to love this island. I dedicate this book to Emily and the people of Gwynn's Island.

Mr. W. D. Jenkins, Mr. Timothy L. Pickle, III, Mrs. Paul D. Williams and the *Gloucester-Mathews Gazette-Journal* lent me valuable support in producing this book.

I thank Mrs. Jean Tanner for sharing her research on Hill's Plantation, and the interviews with islanders on the 1933 storm. Mrs. Eleanor Respess, Margaret Swetnam, Wilford Mitchem, George Fitchett and Milton Murray gave me valuable historic information.

Ann LeVanseller, Mrs. Respess, Mrs. Tanner and Wilford and Edward Mitchem read the manuscript for errors. Any errors that remain are mine.

I also thank Tommy Price for letting me use the photograph he took that is on page 40, and the *Gazette-Journal* for letting me use the photograph that is on page 43.

-David D. Ryan

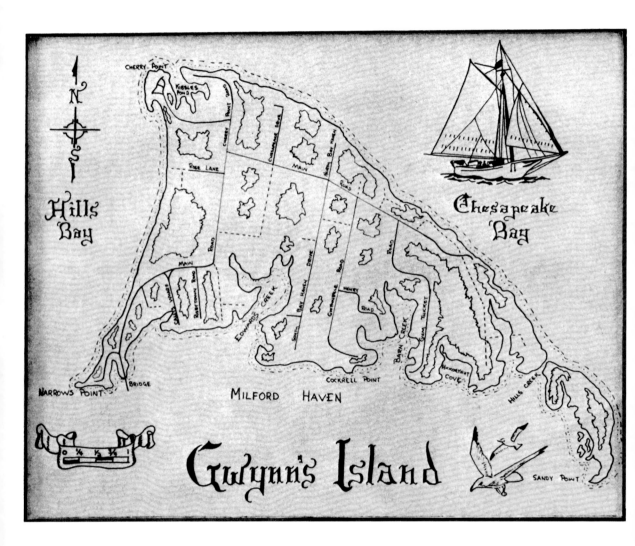

Gwynn's Island

A History

The Name
Gwynn

The storm broke and the sun set the sky on fire.

I penned those words while watching one of the many sunsets I have seen from the beaches of Gwynn's Island. I like to think Hugh Gwynn might have thought that same image more than three centuries ago during his first days on the island he discovered in 1611 while exploring the Chesapeake Bay.

A sunset, or for that matter a sunrise, has romantic qualities and there is a certain romance to the story of the island's discovery.

According to a legend of Gwynn's discovery of the island, he was inspecting the 2,000-acres with two servants when he saw a woman in a small dugout paddling towards them. The water was rough and the frail craft capsized. Gwynn and his servants hastened to the woman's rescue.

Questioning the Indian maiden as to who she was and why she was out in the rough water, Gwynn was reportedly told:

"...I have come to worship the Great Spirit on my island...but you have saved my life (and) I give this island to you in token of my gratitude."

Legends are passed along to be believed or not to be believed. What is true is that Gwynn was granted a charter by the Royal crown for 2,000 acres of the island in 1642 and another 300 acres in 1652.

The grant read:

> Now know ye, that I, the said Francis Moryson, Governor, give and grant, Col. Hugh Gwyn, two thousand acres of land in Gloucester County, at the mouth of the Piankatank River, from Cherry Point to Sandy Point etcl., patent dated 17th day of January 1642, also three hundred acres of residue upon the south west of the said island, being surplussage, patent dated 6th day of January 1652.

Gwynn moved his family of two sons and a daughter to the island where he built a log cabin and named his homestead Gwynnville. The body of water separating the island and the mainland he called "Milford Haven" after a similar body of water in his native Wales.

Little is known of Hugh Gwynn, and there are no portraits of him. But one can imagine he was likely a sturdy man about five feet, six inches tall. His face was probably weathered from the harsh life of frontier living and he likely wore a beard.

The Gwynn family would have had to be self sufficient, living isolated on the island. They would have grown corn and wheat and probably built some type of mill to grind the corn and grain. They would have planted fruit trees—some still exist on the site of Gwynn's property—and canned these and vegetables grown in their garden.

And like present day watermen, the Gwynns would have harvested oysters, crabs and fish from Milford Haven and the Chesapeake Bay.

Gwynn also likely built some type of fortification to protect his home from Indians known to live on the island when he moved there from Jamestown.

The name Gwynn, also spelled Gyn, Gynn, Gwyn, Gwins, Guin and Guinn, is Welsh for white or fair haired. Gwydin or Gwydir Castle in Llanwst, Wales was the home of the Gwynn family.

The July 1778 Harper's Magazine cover featured a windmill on Narrows Point at Gwynn's Island. This painting of the cover is by Grace J. Williams.

Hugh Gwynn was one of the first representatives to the Virginia House of Burgesses from what was then part of Gloucester County.

Gwynn's Island became a part of Mathews County in 1790 when the latter was carved from Gloucester County. The island is located in the Middle Peninsula area of Virginia, 146 miles southeast of Washington, D.C. and 75 miles east of Richmond. The island is two miles long and a mile wide. The year-round population is about 700 residents.

The Gwynn family settled much of the island over the 150 years after its discovery. A second home was built east of Hugh Gwynn's, and a plantation was begun on the Chesapeake Bay side of the island. In addition, the Kibble or Keeble family had moved to the island by 1776, according to a map of the island drawn by Thomas Jefferson that year. And that date—1776— is the second most important in the island's history. It was during the summer of 1776 that the island was taken over by Lord Dunmore.

Gen. Andrew Lewis

Lord Dunmore

John Murray, fourth Earl of Dunmore, England, the last Royal governor of the Old Dominion, cast anchor off Gwynn's Island after setting fire to Norfolk and moving up the Chesapeake Bay with 500 men. Dunmore, a man detested by Virginians, hoped to use the island as a last stronghold from which to incite Virginia slaves to rebel. He landed his men at Narrows Point and along the beaches of Hills Bay. He positioned his ships in Hills Bay and Milford Haven.

The Virginia militia responded to Dunmore's actions by setting up cannon batteries on Cricket Hill on the mainland opposite Narrows Point. A furious battle resulted, and this account was carried in the *Gazette*, a newspaper printed in Williamsburg, on July 29, 1776:

> We got to the island on Monday the 8th, and next morning, at 8 o'clock began a furious attack upon the enemy's shipping, camp and fortifications, from two batteries, one of five, six and nine-pounders. What fources the enemy had, were encamped on the point of the island nearly opposite to our five-gun embrasures, and a breastwork of considerable extent. Besides this, they had two other batteries, and a stockage fort higher up the haven where troops were stationed to

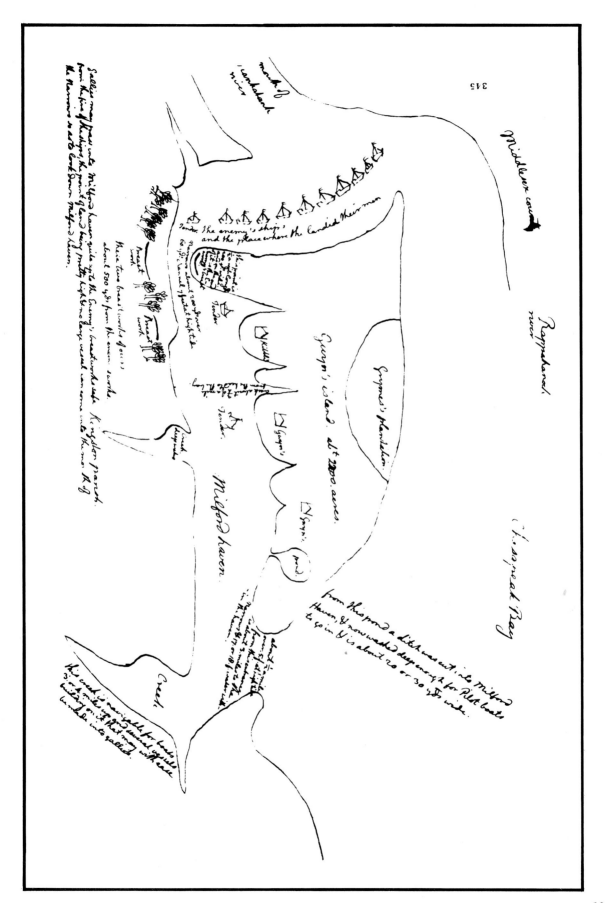

prevent our landing. In the haven (Milford Haven) were three tenders: one a sloop (the Lady Charlotte), mounting six carriage guns; a schooner of two carriages, six swivel guns and cohorn; a pilot boat, badly armed, who had orders from Captain Hammon, of the Roebuck, to prevent our boats passing over to the island, and to annoy the rebels by every means in their power.

Gen. (Andrew) Lewis announced his orders for attacking the enemy by putting a match to the first gun, an eighteen pounder, himself; and the Dunmore (the name of the English flagship) being the nearest to us, at the distance of about 500 yards, it passed through her hull and did considerable damage. Our first gun batteries began playing on the fleet, the enemy's camp, and works; and the fire soon became so hot that the Dunmore was obligated to cut her cables and haul off, after receiving ten shots, some of which raked her fore and aft. The Otter (another of Dunmore's ships) lay next to her, and it was expected would have taken her birth but the first shot we gave her, took place supposed between wind and water, and she immediately slipped her cable likewise, and hauled out of the careen, without firing a gun. By this time all the fleet any way near the shore began to slip their cables in the utmost confusion; and had the wind set in with a floodtide, we must have taken great number of them.

Our eighteen-pounders did great execution from the upper battery, soon silenced the enemy at the point, knocking down several tents, which put their camp into a great confusion. At half after 9 the firing ceased, which was renewed again at 12, with double vigor, from both batteries and nothing prevented our pushing to the island during the cannonade, but the want of vessels (boats to cross Milford Haven).

(The following day, July 9th, the American rebels crossed to the island, using small boats commondeered from local creeks.)

Gen. Lewis, then ordered two hundred men, under Colonel M'Clanahan, to land off the island, which was performed as expeditiously as our small vessels would admit of. On our arrival, we found the enemy had evacuated the place with the greatest precipitation, and were stuck with horror, at the number of dead bodies, in a state of putrefaction, strewed all the way from their battery to Cherry Point, about two miles in length, with a shovel full of earth upon them; others gasping for life; and some had crawled to the water edge, who could only make known their distress by beckoning to us. By the smallpox and other malignant disorders which have raged on board the fleet for many months past, it is clear they have lost, since their arrival on Gwy's Island, near five hundred souls. I myself counted one hundred and thirty graves or rather holes loosely covered...

The American rebels recorded one casualty—a Frenchman who was killed when he fired a gun he had made, which exploded.

Evidence of the Cricket Hill fortifications and cannon batteries can still be found among the trees and grasses east of the Milford Haven Coast Guard Station.

The Keeble House on Cherry Point is believed to have been constructed about 1700.

The Keeble House
and Gwynnville

The two oldest structures on the island are the Keeble House on Cherry Point and the Gwynnville House near Cockrell Point. What few records that exist show both houses were built before the Civil War, and the construction of the houses indicates both date to near 1700.

Stories passed down from family to family say that the Keeble House was built by a sea captain who was believed to be a pirate.

That there were Keebles (also spelt Kibble and Kebble) living on the island as early as 1776 is evident from a map drawn by Thomas Jefferson that year showing Lord Dunmore's occupation of the island. In addition, land records show Keebles or Kibbles owned land in then Gloucester County as early as the 1650s.

(Jefferson's map shows the "Kibble" home located

near Edwards Creek on the southern end of the island. However, this probably was a mistake as Jefferson drew the map based on information he was told.)

The existing Keeble House was constructed in three stages. The earliest part has three evenly spaced windows facing east and facing west on each of the three stories. From the third floor, Captain Humphrey H. Keeble could see over the sand dunes and observe shipping in the Chesapeake and Hills bays.

The size of the house was doubled some years later. The addition is distinct from the original in that there is only one window on the east and west sides on each floor. But the framing in both sections is identical—marked by Roman numbers; dovetailed on the bottom, and held by wooden pins. Each room has a similar fireplace.

Remarkably, the original pane glass in the windows is mostly intact, despite there having been many children raised in the house. The hardwood front door, which originally faced east, bears nails of the kind used by the earliest Colonial carpenters. Anyone over six feet tall has to stoop to enter the doorway.

The pine wood floors show the wear of hundreds of feet that stood, walked and perhaps danced in the rooms. The plaster for the walls was made from ground-up oyster shells, a material used in the construction of many Colonial homes.

The stories handed down from islander to islander say the first island Keeble ran a fleet of square rigged sailing ships from Gwynn's Island to the Mediterranean. He shipped grain and wheat from the island and brought back fruit trees, lumber and other dry goods. Some of the Damson trees Keeble brought from Sicily still grow near the Keeble House.

Across the Cherry Point road and east about 200 yards is the Keeble Cemetery. The dozen headstones are

"Gwynnville" (above), a pre-Civil War house, was built on the site of Hugh Gwynn's estate. Wilford Mitchem (right) lived there for 65 years and rarely left the island until his high school days. (Painting of Gwynnville by Shirley Vreeland).

hidden in a small clump of trees in the center of a field. Several of the tombstones are broken or are too worn to be readable, but most of the inscriptions are discernable.

There are at least three Humphrey H. Keebles buried in the cemetery—one born in 1768, who lived to be 36 years old; the second born in 1800, who lived to be 74 years old, and the third born in 1824, who lived to be 60 years old.

The second Humphrey H. Keeble is listed as "Capt. on the headstone, likely a reference to a ship's officer's title, as all the early Keebles were thought to be seafarers. Sarah C. Keeble, who was born in 1797 and lived to be 71 years old, was his wife. Their daughter, Sarah C., died at the age of 8 years, 2 months and 10 days.

There are also two other Keeble children buried in the cemetery—Robert H., 6 months and 26 days, and Louisa A., 4 months and 13 days. Islanders speculate the children died of malaria, as the Keeble property included a pond whose water frequently became stagnant and bred mosquitoes. (The pond was breached during a storm and is now a cove of the Chesapeake Bay.)

Ellen M. Keeble was born in 1834 and later married John B. Hill of Hill's Plantation. She lived to be 65 years old.

Around the turn of the century, the house was sold and the last of the Gwynn's Island Keebles moved to Middlesex County. Ownership of the house changed hands several times, and the house was put to various uses, including the storage of corn and wheat during the 1920s. About mid century, the house was restored to its original splendor, and a one-and-a-half-story wing with modern conveniences was added on the western side.

Besides the Keeble family, there were four other families living on the island in the early 1800s. According to land records researched by Mathews County resident,

Milton Murray, the families and the land they owned in 1812 were:

Ambrose Adams Family: 35 acres
Gwynn Family: 235 acres
Humphrey H. Keeble: 407 acres
Marchant Family: 50 acres
Hudgins Family: 1,247½ acres

The two-story Gwynnville House was built prior to the Civil War on the site of Hugh Gwynn's property. The house is located at the south end of Gwynnsville Road. It was constructed of redwood and cypress brought by schooner from New England and of local hardwoods, according to Wilford Mitchem, one of the previous owners.

Although most of the records on the house were destroyed during the Civil War, it is known that in 1865 the home was sold to a Dutton Family and that the property included 500 acres, extending from the Chesapeake Bay to Milford Haven. During the war, the house was used to shelter island families whose property was damaged or destroyed during the conflict.

The estate, known as "Gwynnville," was purchased by Dorsey Mitchem in 1907. The original L-shaped porch was deteriorating, so it was replaced.

The three main rooms on the first floor are spacious and have 12-foot ceilings. A fourth smaller room on the west side of the house is used as a kitchen. Fireplaces were used to head each room on both floors. Exposed timbers in the attic are held in place by wooden pins.

There were seven outbuildings when the elder Mitchem bought the property, including a gas house to light the main house, a buggy house, a hen house and a goose house. The elder Mitchem ran a mill on the estate to process grain and corn he and his neighbors raised.

Hill's
Plantation

Still remembered by some of the current residents of the island is a plantation that existed on the southeastern point of the island. It consisted of 328 acres and was owned by Thomas Edwards, "a farmer," in 1850, according to land records. The first name of the plantation is believed to have been "Buck's Chase."

Thirty years later, a census showed the estate was the property of Charles R. Hill, who moved to the island with three servants from New Hampshire. The property was listed on land records as "Hill's Plantation."

Another census taken in 1900 showed the plantation was owned by Charles' brother, John. Tax records indicate the property included a main house and several outbuildings. The house was a three-story, white structure similiar in style to Gwynnville. There were four chimneys, ten to twelve rooms and a porch that extended around the house, according to George Fitchett, 78, who has lived most of his life on Cherry Point. Fitchett recalled that Hill liked to ride throughout the island in a surry.

"He was quite a sight, all dressed up and waving to everyone he saw," Fitchett said.

The heirs of John Hill sold the plantation in the late 1920s. The house burned in March 1931—a spectacular fire that was seen from the bay by fishermen who were returning with their day's catch. The land was later owned by a lumber company and others before being sold for individual home and cabin sites, but the Hill Plantation remains a part of the island lore.

The past of the island is also told in artifacts found on the island and in the water surrounding it. Mrs. Jean Tanner, a "come-here" from Virginia Beach, has

The island's first ferry began in 1884. It was pulled by hand along a cable from Narrows Point to the mainland.

accumulated a small collection of Indian relics, pottery and remains of sea life that date back millions of years.

On loan to the collection is a molar from a Mastodon, an extinct relative of the elephant, that has been dated by state archeological officials to be about 15 million years old. The teeth were dredged from the bay by Dean Close, an island waterman.

Mrs. Tanner has found bison and shark teeth, a fossilized whale vertibrate and a fossilized softshell crab.

Her collection of Indian relics includes a clovis point that is associated with the Paleo Indians who roamed the area about 9000 B.C. Among her most prized finds are a blue and gray jug and a tankard, both of which carry King George III's export initials, "G.R." The stoneware has been identified as being exported by the British to the colonies from Germany until the Revolutionary War.

Pieces of Colonial-era jug were found on the site of Hill's Plantation. "GR" is King George III's export initials.

John T. Loop

The Great
Storm

In 1933 the Chesapeake Bay area was struck by a powerful storm, greater than any in recent memory. Six natives related their experiences on the island during the August 22-23 storm:

Mrs. Eleanor Respess lives on Milford Haven in the same house from which she watched the storm:

"...on the night of August 22, I was sleeping beside a window and the wind was blowing a terrific gale.

"...by mid morning..., the view from this porch was as if you were on the ocean. The water was the color of milk, almost, because of the waves. They would hit the house and break over the kitchen. We had a 42-foot canoe that my father was concerned about and he went out to try to check on it. We could see his head at times. Sometimes we couldn't, because the waves would wash right over him, and my mother was screaming, because she thought something was going to happen to him..."

John T. Loop lives on North Bay Haven Drive:

"On August 23 I got up and looked out the window. I was living in the house next to the Callis's Wharf with Mister (Eugene) Callis. I looked out the window and

R. Stewart Edwards

there was the tide nearly up to the porch! Covered everything down there on the lower end (south end) of the island. We called it the August Gust!''

The late Mrs. Vernon ''Addie'' Rowe, lived on Gwynnsville Road:

''...It got so dark and dreary that the hens and chickens went to roost! They didn't know, but it was a terrible time...''

R. Stewart Edwards, who operates Edwards' Railway, a boat building and repair facility on Edwards Creek:

''My father had a 40-foot canoe, 'Rescue T,' and it broke its stake and went over into Lane's Creek. But as it happened, it got up into a little ditch up there and it was almost damage free. A lot of other boats were lost. Captain Sam Brownley lost one. It busted up at the ice plant (at Callis's Wharf), a total loss and many more. Just a terrible time. Water was up in the houses..., and it was a foot and a half deep right here on Edwards Creek.''

Mrs. Fannie Godsey, 90, who lived for 56 years in a home next to the building that now houses the island's fire department on the main road of the island:

''The houses on Barn Creek had water in them and several people had to be evacuated when the tide came

L. R. "Scrooch" Callis

Mary and Ralph Valdrigi

in. That's the reason they called it a tidal wave. The winds were so strong that when the tide come, it just flooded the banks of the creeks and came up onto the island nearly to the center..."

L. R. "Scrooch" Callis, who operated the Callis's Mercantile Co. on Callis's Wharf at the time of the storm:

"Well, I was living on Risbytown Road and I knew we were having a bad storm of course. Early that morning, possibly about 7 o'clock, my brother, who was captain of the ferry that ran from Callis's Wharf to Cricket Hill, came by and told me that water was in my store.

"...I remember going right on out my front door and running to Callis's Wharf. When I got on the main road, ...you could see the water coming up and the seas were high enough that at one time, it knocked me over... I don't recall how high the water was then, but it must have been more than a foot deep in there (the store), which was unusual...

"When the wind changed, it seemed to blow heavier than ever and the tide rushed back in much higher than it was before. There was a porch on the store. It washed that away...

"I remember...when the storm went on by, you couldn't get in the front door of the store, because the porch was gone...

Mrs. Eleanor Respess and Ling Ling

"I remember some gentleman coming in the back door... He talked for a while and started out (the front door), and ZIP he was gone! Didn't hurt him much though. After that we got boards so you could walk across the drop."

The
Watermen

From Hugh Gwynn's time to the present, the bay has been a major source of food and employment for island people. The earliest boat used to harvest the fish, oysters and softshell and hardshell crabs was a log canoe, much like the Indians used. This canoe was refined to carry sails and is known as a two masted brogan. For many generations, this swift moving, highly maneuverable craft was the taskmaster for the watermen.

A day for the island watermen begins before sunrise when millions of twinkling pinholes of light pierce the curtain of blackness in the sky. George "Buddy" Rowe heads out of Edwards Creek and the water parts in florescent colors from the slicing bow of his boat. The

View from airplane shows Edwards Creek (bottom to top of picture) and Barn Creek.

drum of the engine's pulse thumping in the handle he holds to guide the boat tells him the boat's speed.

The first light of dawn paints the sky pink as Rowe reaches his line of orange corks that mark his crabpots.

His next motions are like synchronized music. He thrusts a pole with a hook at one end and catches the line of the first pot. The line is attached to a motorized pully and the crabpot is wrenched from the bay. The pot is swung onboard where its contents are dumped to the bottom of the boat. Crabs scurry around the waterman's feet, their claws raised and open in defense.

There follows the pot-rebaiting-wire-door-closing-swing-to-the-water-motion and the pot sinks back to the bottom of the bay to again become a trap for crabs.

The motions are repeated seventy-five to a hundred times or more before Rowe turns his boat to head back to an island wharf to sell his day's catch.

Crabbing grew rapidly in the first quarter of this century. In 1929 and 1930 the hard- and softshell crab catches for the bay area of Virginia and Maryland totalled 68 million pounds and 64 million pounds and had a dockside value of $1.7 million and $1.2 million, respectively.

But crabbing is a cyclical business. In 1934 the total catch in pounds dropped to 39 million pounds, while in 1969 an all time record was set at 97 million pounds.

During, fall, winter and early spring months, the watermen turn their efforts to harvesting oysters. And during season, fishing is another important source of income.

But while the sea is vitally important to employment for island residents, others hold land jobs to which they commute throughout the Tidewater area.

Island
Life

Life on the island for Hugh Gwynn and those who followed him was an isolated one. For even though the mainland is a stone's throw away, the island was accessible only by boat until 1939 when a bridge was constructed.

Prior to the bridge, horse-drawn buggies and surrys were kept in sheds on the mainland, and islanders rowed canoes across Milford Haven with their horses swimming behind them.

The late Thomas E. Edwards, a pilot of the island's first ferry, recalled the days before and after the ferries during an interview with the *Gloucester-Mathews Gazette-Journal* in the 1950s.

"I remember that like it was yesterday. When we got to Narrows Point, Daddy and I and my sister would get in

In the past 40 years, Gwynn's Island has been a popular vacation spot for "summer people," many of whom have built cottages like these overlooking the Chesapeake Bay.

the canoe (a double-ended boat, about 20 feet long, propelled by sculling), and Daddy would scull us across while I held the bridle of the horse, who swam behind us. When we got over to the other side, at the original site of Cricket Hill Post Office, about a hundred yards below the present bridge, we would hitch the horse up to the buggy we borrowed at the home of a friend there and would drive to Mathews Court House. When we returned later that day, we would leave the buggy; pick up the canoe, and the horse would swim along behind us on the way back to Narrows Point."

About 1883, when Mr. Edwards was 11 years old, the citizens of Gwynn's Island and the mainland decided that a ferry should be instituted to link the island to the mainland on a more efficient basis.

A group of local men took stock in an organization, and the ferry began to operate in 1884. A steel cable was carried across Milford Haven from Narrows Point to the old Cricket Hill site, and a flat, barge-type ferry boat,

which could carry two buggies and one road cart, was
built by Mr. William Foster and Mr. Charles Hudgins.

"About ten years later, when I was 21 years old," said
Edwards, "I took the job of ferryman for about a month.
I was paid $12 for it and it was the hardest work I ever did
in my life. We had a wooden device with which we
gripped the cable and I would walk to the front of the
boat, then grab this wood on the cable and walk all the
way to the back. Then I would detach the wood, slide it to
the back, then walk up the front of the boat again, and
start again. In other words, we made just one boat length
every time I pulled. Sometimes, when the tide was
running strong, I would have to get the people, who were
riding on the ferry, to help me, because it would even pull
one side of the ferry under a little bit."

Around 1925 a motorized ferry was run from Callis's
Wharf to New Cricket Hill. It could carry three cars on
each side of the pilot house.

The Callis's Wharf ferry was always berthed at the
island after its last run in case one of the islanders
became sick during the night, explained W. D. Jenkins,
an island native. The island had no doctor.

Jenkins tells how, when he was a boy, he and friends
would be hired to sleep on the ferry should it be needed
during the night.

"Some nights some of the island boys would come back
to the ferry landing on the mainland too late to catch the
last ferry. They would honk their car horns to get our at-
tention," Jenkins recalled.

"We would take the ferry across to them and then see
how much they were willing to pay to get back to the
island."

Wilford Mitchen recalls growing up at Gwynnville, the
family home.

Doris Edwards *Mary Ray* *Doris Loop* *Kathy Sadler*

Scrooch's Store, G. R. Clark

The contrast in styles of homes on Gwynn's Island is shown in these three photographs. The Noel E. Loop house (opposite page) and the John Hudgins house (bottom, this page) are typical of homes built in the 19th century in Tidewater, Virginia. The brick house was built by Timothy L. Pickle, III and his wife, Coralan, between 1981 and 1984.

A late afternoon sun plays its light across Gwynn's Island in this view looking northwest from the Chesapeake Bay.

"We were pretty much self-sufficient. You raised everything from your hogs and cows to your vegetables, and much of your other food came from the sea," he said.

Until he went to high school on the mainland, Mitchem said, he didn't much know anyone except his neighbors on the island.

As children, Mitchem, his brother, Edward, and other island boys would imitate their fathers' work as watermen by setting out nets in the water to catch minnows, while their fathers caught fish from pound nets.

"We didn't get to go off (the island) very often. There wasn't much to go off for," Mitchem noted.

George "Buddy" Rowe heads back to the island after emptying his line of crabpots.

Since the island was isolated until 1939, entertainment, in the form of dramas and plays, was brought to the islanders.

Mrs. Respess recalls going down as a child to Callis's Wharf to watch matinee performances put on by members of Adam's Floating Theater, a stage set on a barge that was towed by tug to areas throughout Tidewater during the 1920s and 1930s.

Captain Jim Callis began Callis's Wharf. The road that leads to the buildings at the base of the wharf had been a small inlet that led to Callis's home at the end of State Route 634. The captain's schooner would pull into the inlet and its oyster shell ballast would be dumped into the small body of water.

Slowly a road was built, then a foot dock. In time the wharf was expanded and a seafood processing plant was added. During the 1950s, workers at the plant would pick

*Crabbing is an important source of employ-
ment for island watermen like James Lee Forrest
(opposite page). The crabs are picked (above)
and the meat weighed at the Milford Haven
Seafood Company. Photo opposite page by
Tommy Price.*

A waterman's day ends with the sunset as he readies his boat for the coming morning's chores.

5,500 pounds of crabmeat a week and shuck 200 gallons of oysters a day.

Callis' son, Walter Eugene, later built a much larger dock and added gas and oil facilities. He let the Maryland Steamboat Company use the wharf as a berthing point. During the golden era of waterbound trading, the steamer would stop at the wharf five times a week.

The wharf was sold in 1971 to Milford Haven Seafood, Inc., which still operates facilities there.

There are two post offices on the island; one at Grimstead and the other at Gwynn. Islanders primarily patronize the post office closest to their home, even though the two are within easy walking distance of each other. Through the years, a number of islanders have manned the post offices, including Scrooch Callis. The current postmistress at Gwynn is Mary Ray, who took

During the cold months, the watermen tong for oysters. Les Croxton begins unloading his shellfish at Callis's Wharf.

over the position when Doris Edwards retired in October 1985. Kathy Sadler handles the duties at the Grimstead Post Office, now that Doris Loop has retired.

Through the years there have been a series of grocery and supply stores on the island, but currently there is only one, Scrooch's Market. It is located next to the Grimstead Post Office and is operated by G. R. Clark.

One of the most noticeable landmarks is the Islander Motel and Restaurant and adjacent Narrows Marina—one of the largest such boat facilities in the Middle Peninsula area. The complex was begun in 1969 by Jenkins and is visible on the left as a visitor crosses the bridge to the island.

The island's second restaurant is the Seabreeze, operated since 1979 by Mary and Ralph Valdrighi, "come-heres" from Richmond.

There is also another marina, Pulley's, located since 1965, on a cove of Milford Haven and Edward's Railway on Edwards Creek.

One of the newest businesses is the Plain 'N' Fancy, Manufacturing, operated by Linda and Frank Gallup. The firm has been making handcrafted reproductions since 1979 for museums, catalog houses and shops throughout the country.

Religion has been an important part of the islanders' lives, and the Gwynn's Island Baptist Church stands as a reminder. Located on the main road, the church was organized in 1874 and its present wooden structure with its needle-point steeple was built in the 1920s. It serves more than 300 resident members.

The Gwynn's Island Holiness Chapel (also known as Pilgrim Holiness Church) sits in the woods off Gwynnsville Road. It has a congregation of less than 20.

Islanders also depend on fishing for income.

In the mid 1970s, the church formerly used by the island's Methodist congregation was purchased by the island civic league members. The wooden structure was jacked up and moved by trailer across the main road from its position next to the Baptist church and set on the four-acre Memorial Park, the site of the island's former schoolhouse. The church building is now used as a cultural center by the civic league.

The island has served many warm weather residents for more than 40 years, when the first "summer people" began vacationing there.

Many of the summer people have built cabins or houses overlooking the Chesapeake and Hills bays. In the last 15 years, the summer population has increased with the development of the Gwynn's Island Campers Haven, located on a portion of the site of Hill's Plantation.

For many years the island's name was listed incorrectly on highway signs and maps as Gwynn Island. State officials finally corrected the situation after a letter writting campaign to them by Mrs. Respess. She continues to try to convince the Federal Government to list the correct name on the U. S. Geodetic maps.

Religion is an important part of the islander's life. Children play during summer Bible School (this page). The Gwynn's Island Baptist Church (both pages) was founded in 1874.

The sun sets over yachts berthed at Narrows Marina, one of the largest such facilities in the Tidewater area.

The Islander Motel and Restaurant are located on Narrows Point and are the island's largest landmarks.

*Over the last 15 years, campers have discov-
ered Gwynn's Island and the island campground
provides over 100 year-round and temporary
campsites. Waves left this impression in sand
(opposite page).*

Many graceful sailing craft, such as the one above, use Gwynn's Island as a port of call.

Cattails

Ryan 3/18/84

Green Heron

Cottages along
Hills Bay
David
Flynn
'86

Waterman leaves Milford Haven Seafood Company pier after selling day's catch of Chesapeake Bay Crabs.

Ten years ago, islander, Frank H. Judson, wrote a poem to commemorate the island's July 4th celebration. Following are a few stanzas:

Here's a special southern recipe
Which you will find sublime
This one takes some concentration
And requires a lot of time.

You will find the main ingredients
Way down on Chesapeake Bay
So to make up this concoction
Please turn your thots this way.

Mix up two thousand acres
Of sandy soil and loam,
Roll flat and crimp the edges
Pick a spot to build your home.

Stir in ten thousand pine trees
And a lot of shrubs and flowers
Garnish well with honeysuckle
And let it stand for hours.

Add spice of air and sunshine
Enuf to suit your taste
Take all you want of these two things
There's plenty to waste.

Gwynn's Island, Virginia, A History and Pictorial Essay, is the third book by David D. Ryan, a native of Richmond. A writer and photographer for 30 years, Mr. Ryan's other books are *Harvest of a Quiet Eye* and *The Falls of the James.*